# TAKE A DEEP BREATH... RELAX... CUZ YOU GOT THIS!

*Insights to Motivate, Inspire, and Support You on Your Blended Family Journey*

## Lois Goudeau

The Relatable Therapist

ISBN 979-8-9911150-3-2 (paperback)
ISBN 979-8-9911150-4-9 (digital)

Second printing edition 2024

Published by Gentle Rain Publishing
Contact info: gentlerainpub@gmail.com

Printed in the United States of America

# DEDICATION

*To my husband, Russ, whose strength, continual sacrifice, enduring love, and commitment to us helped me to evolve into a better wife, mom, and stepmom. To our five children: Stephanie, Russ Jr., Jamila, Reuben, and Omari, you all have taught me in ways that I could never have imagined the meaning of unconditional love, acceptance, mutual respect, open communication, and patience. I thank God for giving me the courage to share my life and experience with others on this blended family journey!*

# CONTENTS

# INTRODUCTION

## *So Why Did I Write This Book?*

Someone recently said to me, "You're so open about your blended family journey." I thought about that for a second because, at one point in time, that would not have been my truth. I was just like other Christians. I hid the struggles in my relationships, especially the unpleasant, difficult parts, and I would not dare expose them to the world. I honestly had the fear of others looking at us differently. Even now, I can hear my mama saying, "You shared that? You should not talk about it, just pray about it." That is how I lived my life for so many years. As a Christian, especially an African American Christian, you do not "air out your dirty laundry" but just tell it to Jesus (or your pastor) and wait for everything to be "alright."

The person who made the statement was correct. I decided to share. Now there is an undeniable truth in this. That is, when you start to reveal things about your blended family, you're really putting your life out there for people to judge, examine, have a negative opinion about, and even be very critical about. As I give this a little more thought, I am convinced that putting yourself out there is a courageous thing. The reason I do this, however, is not for accolades, it is because it's a win-win situation. It's a win for me because I'm able to help someone, and it's a win for stepparents everywhere because they're able to see that someone has been where they are and that they "get it" and also understand the uniqueness of the journey ahead of them.

Although it has been twenty-seven years of marriage, I still remember the struggle. I was in the first one to three years into my blended family relationship, and I felt like I had made a huge mistake. How could this have happened? Our courtship was beautiful. My husband was so understanding, gentle, supportive, and loving toward me and my children. We had so much in common that I knew he was my soulmate. He also had kids that I had spent time with, and we all really enjoyed each other. Things were going so well that I just knew it wouldn't be difficult to combine our families. So we got married, and like a ball of yarn, things began to unravel. Although we got along wonderfully beforehand, I didn't anticipate or even understand how difficult the reality would be of trying to combine our two families.

I didn't anticipate how my stepchildren would feel and the difficulty they would have adjusting to their "new normal." I didn't understand what they or my (bio)logical children had lost. I didn't anticipate the guilt my husband would feel each time he had to say goodbye to his children while trying to cultivate a new relationship with me and my kids. I didn't anticipate how the relationship would cause me to feel like I was constantly on an emotional roller-coaster. I didn't anticipate how my children would adjust to their new stepdad, as they still deeply longed for their bio dad.

I didn't realize that our parenting styles would be so different. Nor did I anticipate that effective communication in the blended family had to be learned. I didn't anticipate the intense negative reactions from his ex-partner and the constant struggle over every little decision involving my bonus kids. I truly did not anticipate our peaceful life becoming tumultuous. We began to have so many arguments that it left us both exhausted. I didn't hear him, and he didn't hear me, so we were both constantly frustrated.

Now, don't get me wrong; we had some really good times together overall, and after each argument, we would make up and promise to do better. But after a few months, we'd be back on that same roller coaster. We tried seeing a counselor, but this wasn't a mental health issue, and the counselor had little to no experience in blended family relationships. Although he gave us some useful strategies for stress and anxiety, the sessions weren't very useful in helping us blend our family.

We also tried speaking to our pastor because, after all, we're both Christians. But again, our issues required a level of understanding that just wasn't there. Yes, prayer was good, but we needed more than just prayer. The advice given to us did not address the issues in our relationship, so we struggled more and more as time went on until, eventually, we separated several times. Each time, however, we did reunite because we truly loved each other, and we wanted to make our marriage work.

The first concrete decision we made was to close the door to separate. We needed to start addressing our issues, and though it was painful and took many years of working on ourselves, concurrent with blending our family, we did it.

Now why did it take us years to learn? We learned how not to just survive but to thrive in our blended family. We also learned how to put each other first, communicate better, validate one another, and give each other grace because this journey was new to both of us.

Once we did this, we created a solid foundation for our blended family, and that is the reason I have chosen to author this book. I want to help other stepparents in their blended family journey who still feel they need to present an "image" of what their life should look like. Instead, I want you to achieve the level of success we have.

I have a coaching program called Mosaic Transformation Academy, which was created from years of counseling clients and twenty-seven years in a blended family. During the first year of my coaching program, I did weekly live streams called Motivation

Mondays. They were "energy pills" to uplift, strengthen, and encourage stepparents to overcome the challenges they might encounter in their blended family. I am making these motivations available to you in print to share what I have learned.

Afterward, I've added scripture references to support God's promise for your family and reflection questions so you can think about the important points in the segments as you set goals and priorities, put things in perspective, and problem-solving. This will, indeed, benefit your blended family, so whether you're just starting out in your blended relationship and want to know more about the journey, are newly engaged, or if you're already one to five years in, I encourage you to keep going. It is my sincere desire that after reading this book, you will realize that *you can do this*! So *take a deep breath... relax...Cuz you got this*!

> *Jesus looked at them and said, "With man this is impossible, but with God all things are possible."*
> —Matthew 19:26 (NIV)

# CHAPTER 1

## *Realistic Expectations*

I remember when I was younger (much younger), I would watch Cinderella and think, *I can't wait to meet my Prince Charming. We'll fall in love, and he'll make all my dreams come true.* Well, yeah, right! What a fantasy. I had preconceived notions about what would happen in the future without having a full understanding of relationships. This is what happens many times in a blended family; we have fantasies before getting into a blended relationship. I know I did. My fantasy was, I love him, he loves me, and because we love each other, everything is going to work out fine. By default, the children are going to love one another, and we will all just get along wonderfully. Once we got together, however, I realized that what I had in mind was not the case at all. There are unique challenges in the blended family, and there are things you have no control over.

For instance, a stepparent may wonder, "When will the kids like me?" You may be doing everything you can to make the children like you, but they still don't, or they simply don't want to be around you. That's something out of your control. You may look at your family and say, "What's taking us so long? When other families got together, everything worked out great, but for us, it's taking such a long time." That's how I felt about my blended family after a while. It was taking so long. Yet just like your personal experience, it was out of my control.

Let's talk a bit more about some factors that make up the things we have no control over. I want to address some of them, one thing that may be the age of the children. Statistically, the younger the child is, the easiest it is for them to blend into a family, and the older the child is, it's a little bit more difficult because they understand what's going on. They may still want Mom and Dad to be together, and they may look at you as being the cause of why they're no longer together. Even if you're not a part of that dynamic in their mind, they may think that if you weren't there, Mom and Dad could still be together.

Another situation may be dealing with the issue of a parent that passed away, and the child is dealing with grief. They, in their own way, are trying to learn how to handle their emotions and accept you as their stepparent, and this may be difficult for them. Their parents may have been newly divorced or newly separated, and they're trying to get their emotions together with that. It is difficult because before they have a chance to get used to their "new normal," the two families start to combine. That's something that's out of your control.

Yet another big issue that's out of your control is how your significant other's ex feels about you. The ex may not have wanted the relationship to end, yet it did, so now they are grieving the loss of the relationship and could be very angry and very bitter. They may be very negative in their conversations or words concerning you, and the kids may feed off that negativity and resent you.

TAKE A DEEP BREATH… RELAX… CUZ YOU GOT THIS!

Unfortunately, these are things that are out of your control. However, once you get real about what to expect in your blended family and have realistic expectations, you can walk into it with your eyes wide open, and that's one step closer to making a happy blended family!

# REFLECTION QUESTIONS

*And ye shall know the truth and the truth shall make you free.*
—John 8:32

What fantasy did you have about your blended family relationship?

_____
_____
_____
_____
_____
_____
_____
_____
_____
_____

What can't you control as it relates to your bonus children?

_____
_____
_____
_____
_____
_____
_____
_____
_____

What can't you control as it relates to your significant other's ex?

_____
_____
_____
_____
_____

_____

_____

_____

_____


How do you think changing your expectations will improve your blended family relationship?

_____

_____

_____

_____

_____

_____

_____

_____

_____

_____

# CHAPTER 2

## *I Am Not Doing That!*

As you go along in your blended family relationship, I'm sure the phrase "I'm not doing that!" will come up a lot. I was thinking about things that happened in my own blended family relationship and the challenges that we had, and I remember my husband and I both saying that phrase many times because it felt like the last straw that broke the camel's back. It always seemed like there was one more thing that was expected, one more thing to have to give up, just one more thing to be taken away, and the reply would be, "No! Why do I have to do it? I'm not doing that."

From his perspective, it was the courts. They controlled so much of his life. They controlled his child support payments, visitations, vacations, and his medical. Then his ex controlled his relationship with his kids and how they viewed him because they were young and very impressionable, even if the visits would happen or not happen.

He had no control over how she spent the child support payments, what she did, or what she told the kids about him. So this added to his frustration.

With my ex-partner, I had no control over if he paid child support payments, visited the kids, or even if he made time for them to visit him. Also, as a stepparent, I felt like the finances were out of my control, and the scheduling was already in place, so it was out of my control as well.

There were so many adjustments to make, so anytime he would ask me for or to do one more thing, my answer would be, "No! I'm not doing that," or if I would ask the same, he'd say, "No! I'm not doing that." It had become our common response to yet another sacrifice. At some point, we realized this was about more than just "the straw that broke the camel's back."

This was about communication. We had to let each other know what we were feeling. We realized that there were barriers to us understanding how each other felt, and we had to be honest with ourselves about it. How and what we were feeling sometimes made it hard because we were not used to sitting down with ourselves as individuals and figuring out what "I am really feeling?"

"Why am I so resistant? What is the emotion that I'm feeling?"

After we became clear on what we were feeling personally, we were able to sit down with one another and express those things. "I feel like I'm being taken advantage of," or "I'm feeling like I'm getting the short end of the stick."

Once we did that, things began to change a little more. So once you get real with yourself and sit down with your partner, communication can start, and you will be on your way to successfully blending your family because communication is key.

# REFLECTION QUESTIONS

*Let every person be quick to hear, slow to speak, and slow to anger.*
—James 1:19

What is out of your control that you are letting stress you out?

_____

_____

_____

_____

_____

_____

_____

_____

_____

_____

How effective is your communication with your partner?

_____

_____

_____

_____

_____

_____

_____

_____

_____

_____

Are you effective in expressing your true emotion, or do you need to explore it more?

_____

_____

_____

_____

_____

TAKE A DEEP BREATH... RELAX... CUZ YOU GOT THIS!

_____
_____
_____
_____
_____

How do you think this will improve your blended family relationship?

_____
_____
_____
_____
_____
_____
_____
_____
_____
_____

# CHAPTER 3

## *How Are You Blending Your Family?*

I remember when I started out in my blended family. I wanted things to really work; I wanted the family to come together, and it seemed like it was just taking so long to do so. One of the things that I realized is that I was comparing my family to a traditional family, and they are totally different. If you try to compare your blended family to that of a traditional one, you will always feel like you're a failure.

The first step in building your family is to have patience, especially with yourself. This is a totally different journey, one that you've never been on, so you have to have patience with yourself. I heard somebody compare the blended family to a Crock-Pot. You know what? That makes a lot of sense. Think about it. In a Crock-Pot, there are different ingredients put together and cooked slowly so that everything can blend together and won't lose its flavor or its characteristics. If you think about your family as a Crock-Pot meal, then you will realize and accept that it's going to take time. Time to blend each other's personalities to bond, understand each other's behaviors, create traditions, learn cohesive parenting styles, set realistic expectations, and so much more so that everything can blend together authentically. That's why I said that the first step is patience. Patience with yourself to understand that this is going to take time. Some days you'll feel like you hit it on the mark, and other days you'll feel like, "Man, I just really messed up." During those times, give yourself compassion language.

Think about this. If your friend came up to you, and they felt bummed out, like they messed up, you'd be compassionate with them. You'd say something like, "That's *okay*! Yeah, you messed up, but you can try again." You may even remind them of the good things they've done. So give yourself that same compassion language.

Ron Deal wrote a book called *The Smart Stepfamily*, and in it, he compared blended families to kitchen appliances. For instance, he said the "Microwave Stepfamily" has high expectations and attempts to operate like a traditional family. The parents have blinders and do not want to be referred to or identified as a stepfamily and don't recognize the unique challenges of blending a family. Consequently, underlying issues aren't addressed and may lead to dysfunction in the family.

Then there's the "Blender Stepfamily." The members of the family are mixed together very quickly to create a new and improved family. They disregard each other's past, and it also erases important aspects of each member.

Finally, there is the "Pressure Cooker Stepfamily." This family forces the kids to accept the new family unit, including calling the stepparents, "Mom and Dad." This causes stress, and emotions are very high.

When you understand there is a lot that goes into blending a family, having patience is not an option, but it's the most important ingredient.

# REFLECTION QUESTIONS

*Let us not become weary in doing good, for at the proper*
*time we will reap a harvest if we do not give up.*

—Galatians 6:9

Which appliance would accurately define your blended family?

_____

_____

_____

_____

_____

_____

_____

_____

_____

Do you need to adjust your expectations about anything in your blended family?

_____

_____

_____

_____

_____

_____

_____

_____

_____

What compassion language do you need to say to yourself about blending your family?

_____
_____
_____
_____
_____
_____
_____
_____
_____
_____

How will this improve your blended family relationship?

_____
_____
_____
_____
_____
_____
_____
_____
_____
_____

# CHAPTER 4

## *Why Don't My Stepkids Like Me?*

It can be challenging to be around someone that doesn't like you and that has no problem expressing it. But for some reason, it hits differently when it's a child that doesn't like you, especially your stepchild. It makes you feel really bad, and you start to question, "What's wrong with me?" There is one thing I want you to know. This happens in a lot of blended families. The stepchild doesn't like the stepparent, and it's normal for them not to like them right away. Yes, that's right.

There are many reasons for it. First, you have to know that not liking you doesn't have a lot to do with you at all. It has to do with them, their emotions, what's going on in their life at that moment, the stability, and how the consistencies they have known have been completely wiped away. You are just a part of the puzzle of what's going on in their life. I mean, their life has changed, and even if their parents have been separated or divorced for a period of time, you're going to be the reason. You're the one that they're going to take all their frustrations out on. So, in essence, you're the one with the target on your back. Know that they have a lot of things going on.

Again, they're trying to process their emotions and their feelings. As a matter of fact, sometimes, no matter how wonderful you are, they don't care. They don't care if you (1) make everyone happy, or (2) if their parent truly loves you. None of that matters to them. All they know is that when you came into their lives and took on the role of their stepparent, nothing was the same for them. Their world has been turned upside down, and now they must get used to another type of life.

They can't take their frustrations out on their parents because they love them, and so sometimes, you're just the most convenient person, and you're the target. Remember that, and also remember that they may look at you as the reason why they don't get to spend time with their parents. They may look at you as taking their parent away from them.

So that's a couple of reasons why they may say, "I don't like you."

Yet comes another reason. I've talked about this before in my Facebook group, but it is that their bio parent may be influencing them to dislike you. If they want to please their bio parents, even if they do like you, they're not going to show it. This is because they feel like they're torn between their bio parent and you.

I want you to also think about another possibility. As a stepparent, sometimes you may feel isolated and alone. You may feel that you're not the first priority. You may feel like your needs aren't being met, but as strange as it sounds, they feel the same way that you do. When you feel like you're alone in the relationship, no one is listening to you, you're not a priority, and your feelings aren't being considered, just think about how they feel.

So I am going over that with you just to remind you that you have to really think about how your stepchild feels. Put yourself in their shoes and try to look at it from their perspective. Remember, you agreed to be in this relationship. You said that you were going to step up.

They didn't have a choice in the matter, so it's going to take time to process all of this and decide how they feel about you. It may take weeks, or it may take months.

Now that you understand a little bit more about what's going on with your stepkids, and you know it's going to take time for a bond to take place, know that there are things that you can do to start this bonding. I'm just going to talk about a couple of things that you can do. If they're teenagers, respect their space and their boundaries. For teenagers, that's a big deal because they're coming into their own, so to speak. They're trying to figure out who they are, establishing their independence. So you need to respect their boundaries and their space and be respectful. Before you start giving advice, ask them, "Is it *okay* if I share this with you?" or "Is it *okay* if I talk with you about that?" Ask them first before you jump in and start giving your thoughts. If they say something rude, or if they say something that's hurtful to you, don't let them know it. They may use that again the next time they talk to you. What you want to do is have a response already set up for them. "I'm sorry you feel that way," "Let me think about that. I'll get back to you," and "How can I change that?"

Having a response like that makes them feel you're listening to them and that their feelings are important. Then they process what you said and may not come back with an attitude because you're validating their feelings, and again, that's a big deal with them.

Another thing that you can do that's really important is take time to bond with your stepchild and continue to have family connections. Again, if it's a teenager, ask them what they would like to do as a family activity instead of always making suggestions. Say, "Hey, what would you like to do" because you're trying to get their input; you're trying to pull them in to let them know that they are a part of the relationship with you and that it's not one-sided.

You can also think about coming up with some new family traditions. They may already have traditions with their own bio parents that they won't feel comfortable doing with you. So you come up with some new traditions that you can do with them like maybe Friday will be pizza night if you get them over the weekend. Think of something that you and they can do together. I know this seems contrary because they don't like you, so they don't want to be around you, but the only way you're going to be able to begin to bond with them is to spend time with them. That's how bonding takes place.

Here's another thing you can do that is important: show interest in the things that they're doing. If there's a favorite hobby, you can sit down with them and work on that, or if they have a sport they play, you can go out and cheer them on and let them know that you're there for them.

Let them know that you want to listen to them and that you're genuinely interested in the things that they're interested in, and the bottom line is you just have to communicate with them.

Let them know that this is a new area for you as well and that you know they're struggling and that you're struggling too, but you want to be fair and respectful of them. Ask them what are some things that you can do that could help the situation in the relationship.

# REFLECTION QUESTIONS

*And over all these virtues put on love which binds them all together.*
—Colossians 3:14

What challenges you the most as it relates to your stepchildren?

_____

_____

_____

_____

_____

_____

_____

_____

_____

_____

As you think about your stepchild(ren), what issues are they struggling with?

_____

_____

_____

_____

_____

_____

_____

_____

_____

_____

Does understanding their struggle help you be more forgiving of their behavior?

_____

_____

_____

_____

_____
_____
_____
_____
_____
_____

How will changing your perspective improve your blended family relationship?

_____
_____
_____
_____
_____
_____
_____
_____
_____
_____

# CHAPTER 5

## *Is This an Ultimatum or Changing a Behavior?*

As I stated earlier, I am an educator as well as a therapist and coach. Sometimes my stepparents have behavioral challenges with their stepchildren. So I educate them on understanding the difference between an ultimatum and a modification of behavior. To do this, I ask them this question, "Is this an ultimatum, or is it changing my child's behavior?" Many times, parents think that they're changing their child's behavior when actually they're issuing them an ultimatum.

For a working definition, an ultimatum is when you want to change the behavior immediately, and you offer a threat. Parents tend to do this because they're desperate. They become desperate when they're in a situation, uncomfortable, or a rush. For example, imagine that your child is with you outside the grocery store, and they won't get in the car. Everyone is looking at you, and now you're starting to feel desperate, so you say to them, "Either get in the car or I'm going to leave you." Well, we all know you're not leaving your child, but you say it, wanting a behavior to happen immediately. You might also say, "Either get in the car, or when you get home, you won't get any dinner." Again, you're desperate, and you want an immediate change, so you give a threat, an ultimatum.

Now, changing behavior is different; it's called behavior modification. You're trying to change the undesirable behavior and trying to modify it, with some type of process or method over a period of time. You're either trying to decrease or increase something. The key-words to notice are *process* and *method*.

There are four different types of behaviors to modify, and they fall under two categories, discipline and reinforcement. Let me give you examples of both. Under discipline, there's a negative punishment. Let's just say your child isn't doing their homework, and you want them to do it, so as a negative punishment, you said, "Either you do your homework, or I'll take away your electronic device." If that's what you're using as a punishment, that would be negative because there's a punishment for a behavior that you're trying to change.

Another example would be a positive punishment. You might be wondering, "How can a punishment ever be positive?" Well, think about the word *positive* as you're adding a consequence, and it's a positive consequence. For instance, let's just say that your child is bullying another child, so you want that to stop. You would say to them, "You're going to write a letter to this child that you're bully-ing." It's positive because the consequences are positive, but it's still a punishment because it's not something that your child wants to do. That's an example of discipline, negative punishment, and positive punishment.

Now, let's look at reinforcement, it is a behavior your child is doing, and you want them to continue doing it. So you could either praise them with, "I'm so happy you're doing your homework, keep up the good work," or you could give them a positive consequence, such as, "You did your homework, so now you get twenty extra min-utes to play on your electronic device today."

Even though an ultimatum is given out of frustration and des-peration, it may work, but it will only be for a short period of time.

With behavior modification, you want to give them something that will continue over time. For this to happen, there have to be some specific things in place. One thing that has to happen is consistency. You can't give them a punishment or consequence one time and then the next time do something different. For instance, if you give them a timeout for the behavior, and the next time they do that behavior, you're not consistent and may say, "I'm tired. I don't feel like doing it, just go do whatever you want." Behavioral modification isn't going to work because you're not being consistent.

The next thing that has to happen is for the adults to be on the same page. Whether it's the adults in the house or if they're going to the grandparents' house or whoever the other adults are who play a role in their lives. You all have to be doing the same thing and agree on the same thing. If this is going to happen, then it has to happen at their grandparents' house, Dad's or Mom's house. There has to be that consistency and that agreement with the adults.

The last thing that has to happen is some type of consequence or punishment that fits the child when the behavior is displayed. So let's just say if your child could care less about electronic devices, you should know that taking one away from them is not going to work as a negative punishment. They don't like electronic devices anyway, so it doesn't matter to them. Let's say they love books instead. They love really getting caught up in the mysteries of romance books. To take those for a period of time would be a punishment that would be effective. So you have to find out what's going to be effective for each child.

# REFLECTION QUESTIONS

*Discipline your children and they will give you peace;*
*they will bring you the delights you desire.*

—Proverbs 29:17

How do you approach behavior issues with your stepchildren?

_____

_____

_____

_____

_____

_____

_____

_____

_____

_____

Do you think this approach will change their behavior? Have you seen success with that approach?

_____

_____

_____

_____

_____

_____

_____

_____

_____

_____

Are you and your significant other on the same page with consequences? Do you feel working with someone to facilitate your issues will help you?

_____

_____

_____

_____

_____

_____

_____

_____

_____

_____

How will getting on the same page with parenting your stepchildren will improve your blended family relationship?

_____

_____

_____

_____

_____

_____

_____

_____

_____

_____

# CHAPTER 6

## *The Language Decision*

When you start off in the blended family, this question will eventually come up, "Do I want to be called the stepparent?" In the fairy tale, Cinderella had a stepmom and stepsiblings who were wicked, and they would always try to undermine her and always try to make her look bad. They really just hated her. So in society, the word *stepparent* has a negative connotation, and you're faced with what I like to call, "the language decision."

I remember when my kids were little, one of the things that I desperately wanted them to do was to know who I was and to call me Mama. Because of that desire, when they were toddlers, I would work with them to say "Mama." That gave me a sense of belonging and importance in their life. I wanted them to distinguish me from the grandma, the aunt, and any other caregiver. I wanted them to know who I was, and the day they said "Mama," I was just so excited and ecstatic because I knew that they knew who I was. Just as they are very important in a traditional family, titles are important in a blended family as well. Titles matter for the sake of identity in relationships.

One troubling trend that I have seen is that sometimes in blended families, one of the partners will try to force the kids to refer to them as Mama or Daddy. It's troubling because that could put the child in a very uncomfortable position, especially if that position is already taken by their bio parents. It could cause conflict with the other bio parent for you, the stepparent, to try to force their child to call you the mom or the dad. They may be feeling like, "This is my position."

So be considerate in this area. You never want to put the children in an uncomfortable position. The closer you are in the relationship, the more natural it will flow. They may not call you Mom or Dad but another term of endearment. I suggest you sit down with your bonus children and your significant other and find out what they want to call you. Let them take the lead. It should be something you are comfortable with and what they are comfortable with. As long as it's not anything negative, it'll be okay.

In my blended family, the one thing I did do correctly was to allow my children to be comfortable calling their stepdad a term of endearment, and it has stuck to this day.

# REFLECTION QUESTIONS

*Let us search and examine our ways.*
—Lamentations 3:40

Do you struggle with being called a stepparent? Is it a negative word to you?

_____

_____

_____

_____

_____

_____

_____

_____

_____

_____

If they did not call you Mom or Dad, would that bother you? If so, why?

_____

_____

_____

_____

_____

_____

_____

_____

_____

_____

Would it cause a conflict with the bio parent if you were called Mom or Dad?

_____
_____
_____
_____
_____
_____
_____
_____
_____
_____

If you allow the stepchildren to take the lead on what they call you, how will it improve your blended family relationship?

_____
_____
_____
_____
_____
_____
_____
_____
_____
_____

# CHAPTER 7

## *Stepping into Your Child's Shoes*

So I want to talk to you about stepping into your child's shoes. This is a topic I believe a lot of people do not think about when they talk about a blended family. It is looking at the situation from the child's point of view.

I know a lot of people may say to a child in a blended family, "Look at all the things you've gained by being in this wonderful, blended family," but have you ever thought that the child may have a sense of loss because they have lost so much? The family that they had, and what normal feels like. Now they are in this blended family with new people and depending on the age of the child, their position in the family may have changed. They cannot even acknowledge or understand their emotions. They may have lost their grandparents because the situation became so volatile that one side of the family is not speaking to the other side of the family. They may have lost traditions that they once held with their family. They have lost the routine that they were used to, and now they must learn a whole new parenting style.

As you can see, there are a lot of things that the child has lost when they come into a blended family. When someone experiences a loss, it is called grief, and grief is tough for anyone. Sometimes when a child is having a behavioral issue, it may not just be that, but it may be because of grief. Since they do not know how to fully express how they feel, a preschooler and a toddler may start having tantrums. As a parent, you do not know what is going on, so you may think they are having a behavior problem or they are just not listening; they do not want to do what you tell them to do. They could be grieving, but it shows up as a tantrum.

Children may go back to bed wetting, sucking their thumbs, or going back to a number of things that they have recently graduated from. Now they are back to doing them because they have emotions that are showing up but are not understood to be grief.

Teenagers may feel like they cannot control their life. When it looks like they are not listening, they are being disobedient, or they do not want to do what the other parent is telling them, it may also be grief. Look at it from the child's point of view and not just assume that they are having a negative behavior moment. They may also be having a sense of loss.

Think about a bio mom. She must learn and come to understand her new child and figure out what her child's crying behavior means. Is the child wet, hungry, or tired? That is what you have to do with your new bonus children. You must get to know them, and by knowing them, you will understand if they are going through grief. If they are, figure out what you need to do as a stepparent to help them through that grieving process.

# REFLECTION QUESTIONS

*Accept one another; just as Christ accepted you.*
—Romans 15:7

What losses do my bonus children have?

_____
_____
_____
_____
_____
_____
_____
_____
_____
_____
_____

What behaviors are associated with their losses?

_____
_____
_____
_____
_____
_____
_____
_____
_____
_____
_____

How can you help them through it?

_____
_____
_____
_____
_____
_____

_____

_____

_____

_____


How will it improve your blended family relationship?

_____

_____

_____

_____

_____

_____

_____

_____

_____

_____

# CHAPTER 8

## *Vulnerability Helps Your Relationship Grow Stronger*

Thinking back to when I started in my blended family, I felt that I couldn't be emotionally honest with my husband about what I was feeling. I would always blame him, and I felt that he should know and figure out things. I was always putting the ownness on him to know how I was feeling without even talking to him about them. I felt my actions or my nonverbal communication should have been enough. I would always tell him, "You should know." I realized that it wasn't his issue; it was really mine. I was afraid to be vulnerable in our relationship, and that may be happening in your relationship as well.

You're not telling your husband or your partner exactly how you feel because you don't know how they're going to react if they know. The truth is, however, when you're vulnerable in your relationship, it will actually cause that relationship to become stronger. When you choose to put yourself out there, you're letting the person know it's okay, and that allows that other person to be vulnerable as well. This really does help the relationship.

When you're feeling like you're not valued or not appreciated, and even if you feel like you're being left out when you're with your bonus children, that's one of the things you can talk to your spouse about. As I said, there were things my husband didn't even know, and when we talked years later, there were things that I didn't know he felt either. We didn't even know how the other felt because we never communicated that to each other.

So I'm saying to you that your partner may not know how you're feeling. They may not know that you're feeling left out, like a third wheel, isolated, and overlooked. One such example is regarding Mother's Day for me. Although my husband would buy me things on that day because he wanted me to know that he appreciated all I did for my bonus children, he still didn't know how I was feeling inside. I hadn't shared those things with him.

I'm saying to you, share how you are feeling with your partner. It's not just women; my husband wasn't vulnerable on some things either. Sometimes, as people, we don't share things, and we want people to figure it out, but if you don't share it with them how, will they know how you're feeling?

Communicating will help the relationship grow stronger, and it will connect you together on a different level with your partner.

# REFLECTION QUESTIONS

*A gentle answer turns away wrath, but a harsh word stirs up anger.*
—Proverbs 15:1

Do you feel you communicate your feelings effectively with your spouse?

_____

_____

_____

_____

_____

_____

_____

_____

_____

_____

What is an area of vulnerability you have not shared with your partner/spouse?

_____

_____

_____

_____

_____

_____

_____

_____

_____

_____

How have you tried solving your communication issues?

_____

_____

_____

_____

_____
_____
_____
_____
_____
_____

How do you think this will improve your blended family relationship?

_____
_____
_____
_____
_____
_____
_____
_____
_____
_____

# CHAPTER 9

## *Stressed-Out Stepparent?*

Those of you who were parents before you became a stepparent know how stressful it is being a parent, especially if you were a single parent. All the demands that are on you, and even when you don't want to, you have to be fully present. When you are tired because there's nobody else there to help out, you have to continue to be involved in sports, extracurricular activities, parent-teacher conferences, and your child's hobbies. You had to be there to read to them, comfort them, and do all of the other things that you know you have to do as a single parent.

Now, when you step into the role of a stepparent, you still have all of those things that you were doing. With stepchildren, you have more responsibility on your plate. You have to be involved in their lives to get that bond. When you're in the first one to five years of joining your blended family, you have to work on creating that bond, and sometimes, unconsciously, you try to function as a traditional family. Even though you say you understand that blending a family is different than a traditional nuclear family, a lot of times, you function like that. That's why you get burnt out.

So let's just say that you're in your blended family relationship, and as a mother, you do all of the scheduling. If your stepchildren live with you, you're still trying to do the same thing, all of the scheduling. Now you already have your bio children, and now you're trying to coordinate the schedule with your stepchildren as well. Those schedules become much more difficult because you have to involve the other bio parent. Everyone's schedule needs to sync, which can be difficult.

Now, what if there is a parent conference, and you need to navigate the schedule and go to the parent-teacher conference? Then they have all the hobbies that you're trying to be involved in. There are the sports that you're trying to be involved with, the bond you're trying to build with the kids that may not like you, and they still may not want to listen to you. You're still trying to juggle all of that, and it becomes stressful.

You're trying to juggle all of these balls at one time. So can you understand why you're overwhelmed? What I find interesting is if a bio mom says she is stressed out with her kids, no one says anything; everyone actually understands. But as a stepparent, when you say you're stressed out with your stepkids, everyone looks at you like, "Oh my God, what do you mean you're stressed out?" It seems like they think you should never get overwhelmed or stressed. If a bio parent can get stressed out with their kids, don't you think a stepparent can get stressed out with their stepkids too? When trying to create a bond and learning more about your stepkids, it can sometimes feel like you're being pulled and tugged in all directions. Sometimes all of that can become stressful for the stepparent.

Here are some things that you can do to reduce your stress. First, consciously remember that you're trying to create those bonds and blend into a family, and that takes time. Next, recognize if you're taking on too much responsibility. When you're in a blended family, it's not just you, your partner is in it too. They're the bio parents, so let them be involved with their child. After school, let them do the homework with them. Although the father may come home later in the day, it is still his bio child. He can spend time helping with the homework. Instead of you creating all the activities when the kids come over, there's nothing wrong with having a daddy-son night or mother-daughter night. Let the bio parent spend more time with their child.

If you're the stepparent, you don't have to do all of it with the kids. You don't have to think, *All of this is expected of me.* No, you pull back and allow him or her to spend that time with their bio parent, even with parent-teacher conferences. It's not important that you show up, but let the bio parents go to the parent-teacher conferences. Yes, you're a part of their lives, and when he or she comes home, they'll tell you what they talked about. This is good enough; also, it decreases stress if you know that the other bio parent may have an issue with you being there. If you know there may be a conflict, why are you trying to communicate with them? Let their ex-partner communicate with them.

A lot of times, we're inserting ourselves as if it's like a traditional family, and then we're getting stressed out. You're wondering, *Why am I so stressed out?* I need you to remember, again; it's going to take time for those bonds to be created. Just as every traditional family is different, so is every blended family. Yours may look different. So that bio parent doing most of the heavy lifting when it comes to your bonus kids is okay. It's not anything set in stone that says because you are the stepparent, you have to be the one to pack all the sandwiches or you have to be the one to attend all of the events. It's okay! Let that bio parent do that.

# REFLECTION QUESTIONS

*Do not be anxious about anything but present your requests to God.*
—Proverbs 4:6

How has your life changed since being in a blended family relationship?

_____

_____

_____

_____

_____

_____

_____

_____

_____

_____

What responsibilities can you give to your partner or spouse so you can be less stressed?

_____

_____

_____

_____

_____

_____

_____

_____

_____

_____

How will this improve your blended family relationship?

_____

_____

_____

_____

TAKE A DEEP BREATH... RELAX... CUZ YOU GOT THIS!

_____

_____

_____

_____

_____

_____

# CHAPTER 10

## *Keep Your Eyes on the Prize—Us!*

The lyrics "Keep your eyes on the prize" was used during the civil rights movement. The purpose of that song was to remind people that no matter what you were going through, the challenges or struggles, keep their eyes on what is important. Today I'd like to encourage you with the words of that song to keep your eyes on the prize.

A strong family is built on a strong foundation, and that foundation is the parents. Sometimes in a blended family, we get so busy and preoccupied with the children that we make the children the focal point and the foundation of the family, and that will never do. You can't build a foundation on children. One of the things you have to remember is to prioritize the parents.

There is another song with the lyrics "What about us?" If you continue to keep those songs in your mind, "Keep your eyes on the prize" and "What about us," it will remind you of the reason you got together in the first place. You got together because you both loved one another and because you wanted to be with one another. You want to, as some people say, "do life together" and build memories together.

One thing to keep in mind is that one day, the children won't be there. It'll be you two and that life that you planned together. You can still have it, but you have to prioritize each other.

I remember when my husband and I were starting to blend our family, we realized that we had to spend time together. We had to spend time to recharge, reconnect and refuel with one another. We had, what we call, Friday date nights, and we had that time set aside with each other.

So I'm encouraging you today, don't forget about you two. Remember to prioritize each other. There are little things that you can do that will make a big difference. For us, it was date night, and for you, it might be date night too, but there are other things that you can do as well. You can send text messages throughout the day and just put a little emoji to remind your partner that you're thinking about them. Another thing that you can do to let them know "I'm prioritizing you" is that when you see them doing something that you're really feeling proud of, that you're happy about, and that makes you feel good, give them that verbal praise. When we recognize kids, it is called intentional behavior, and with each other, you have to have that intentional behavior also.

The last thing that you can do is remember that your partner is important, so get their opinions first on something that's going to directly impact the family. Ask them their opinion about it so they'll know they are a priority.

# REFLECTION QUESTIONS

*I have found the one whom my soul loves. I
held him and would not let him go.*
—Song of Solomon 3:4

What are some things you are putting before each other?

_____
_____
_____
_____
_____
_____
_____
_____
_____
_____
_____

How can you prioritize each other in the relationship?

_____
_____
_____
_____
_____
_____
_____
_____
_____
_____
_____

How will this improve the blended family relationship?

_____
_____
_____
_____
_____

TAKE A DEEP BREATH… RELAX… CUZ YOU GOT THIS!

_____
_____
_____
_____
_____

# CHAPTER II

## *Give Yourself Permission to Pause*

Sometimes you have to give yourself permission to pause everything that's going on in your life. This pause is self-care. That's not something that's talked about a lot in the blended family; I know that's a "buzzword" for mental health, but in a blended family, it should not be an option because it's vital, and it's necessary when you just stop and think about all the things that you're doing in the blended family. First of all, you're trying to learn how to bond with your bonus child or your stepchild, and then all of the challenges; you may have tried to do that since you have your stepchildren or bonus children on the weekends, or you may have them daily, and that can be very stressful as you're trying to learn their personalities. You're trying to deal with the ex and other extended family members. There might be custody issues and parenting plans in place with their school schedules, and you're trying to juggle all of this, so with all of that going on, having self-care is not optional, but it is vital in the blended family.

Michelle Obama, our former first lady of the United States, had a quote, and I just want to share it with you; it says, "To be a good parent, you need to take care of yourself so that you have the physical and emotional energy to take care of your family." Now this quote can go for anyone, whether you're in a blended family or not, but the key phrase that she said was to "take care of yourself so you have the physical and emotional energy to be able to give out to the rest of the members of your family," and that's the reason why self-care is so important because if you don't take care of yourself, then you don't have anything to give to anyone else, and a lot of times, in the blended family, we're so busy making sure everyone else is taken care of.

We're so busy looking at who needs what and making sure other people's needs are being met. It's very easy to just overlook your own needs, and sometimes, the only time we really realize that we need some self-care is when we are already drained, and we just can't go any longer, so when you feel that way now, it feels like you're depleted. One of the things I remember when I think about self-care is growing up. I never really saw my mother do self-care; I would see her sacrificing for the family and just keep going and going and going (like the energizer bunny), self-care wasn't something she routinely does for herself, so sometimes, when you think about taking time for yourself, you may feel a little guilty, like I shouldn't be enjoying myself because of one thousand other things that need to be done. There's laundry to be folded, those clothes to be washed, there are dishes to be washed, there are floors to be swept and mopped, and it's like this never-ending list, so sometimes you may feel guilty that I have so much to do that I shouldn't take time for myself when you give yourself the permission to do self-care.

You're giving yourself time to pause and also saying I need time to breathe, which, in turn, will help prevent burnout. There's an analogy that I like, and it's called the "ripped clothing analogy," and there are a lot of different other analogies. You've probably heard of one about being on an airplane, and if you don't put the mask on yourself first, you can't help anybody else. There's another one about pouring water from an empty pitcher; if you give out everything, you don't have anything for yourself, but I saw this one about ripped clothing, and I thought a lot of people could relate to this one, so just think about when you have a rip in your clothes.

At first, it is probably small, no one sees it, and it's not that big of a deal, but over time as you move and cause friction, it starts to wear and tear, and a hole appears, and the hole starts getting bigger and bigger and bigger, and coincidentally, I'm thinking about socks because, for me, that's what always gets me is a hole in my sock, and when the hole is little, I don't pay any attention to it. It's like, "Oh, I can see my toenail through the little hole in the sock," but over time, it gets bigger and bigger and bigger to the point that that sock becomes uncomfortable, and it makes it hard for me to be comfortable when I'm walking in it.

Yes, I can walk, but it's uncomfortable. That's the way it is for self-care sometimes; we know we need it, but we just keep pushing and pushing, and then at some point, we start to really feel the pressure, and we start to really get stressed. If you're stressed out, you're not giving the best that you have to your blended family; that's why self-care is so important because, at some point, it begins to lead to physical and emotional stress, and you feel drained and then just think about it when you know that you need to take care of yourself.

Everything gets on your nerves; every little thing the kids do and every little thing your husband or partner says gets on your last nerve. They could have done that before, but now this time, it just irritates you. It just really gets to you, and that's when you need to start to exercise self-care. When we talk about self-care, sometimes some people think you have to join a gym or an expensive spa, but you don't. You can do self-care with inexpensive things. My mom loved working in her yard when we were younger, and we had a huge garden where we grew our own vegetables, and coincidentally, I hated it; I'm just going to tell you now that I hated picking weeds out of it and chasing the varmints so they wouldn't eat it.

Now that I think about it, that was her self-care, and even now, she loves to just sit and watch her flowers digging and planting them in it, and I asked her, "Mom, why do you like being outside?"

She said that's my therapy. She doesn't call it self-care; she calls it her therapy, and it can be an inexpensive activity that you do for self-care. It doesn't have been a long period of time, but it could even be five minutes, ten minutes, or at the end of the day, just enough time for you to take that pause and to be able to just refresh yourself. I like going on vacation that charges me and that gives me energy. I love spending time with my family. I also like reading a book because it takes me to another place; for me, that's my self-care.

Even when your stepkids come over let the bio parent interact with them and you go take that self-care. It's okay to take some time away because if there's a stressful situation, you need to pull away from it, and that's *okay* to let the bio parent spend time with their children, and you can use that time for self-care.

# REFLECTION QUESTIONS

*Beloved I wish above all things that thou mayest prosper
and be in health even as thy soul prospereth.*

—3 John 2

Which analogy will you use to encourage your self-care?

_____
_____
_____
_____
_____
_____
_____
_____
_____
_____

What are some things you do for your self-care?

_____
_____
_____
_____
_____
_____
_____
_____
_____
_____

How often will you incorporate it into your schedule?

_____
_____
_____
_____
_____

_____
_____
_____
_____
_____

How will this improve the blended family relationship?

_____
_____
_____
_____
_____
_____
_____
_____
_____
_____

# CHAPTER 12

## *Holiday Best or Holiday Stress*

The holidays are a wonderful time of the year, but in a blended family, you can either experience holiday stress or holiday best. While growing up, I remember the holiday seasons being festive and full of joy, family gatherings, laughter, and sheer excitement! My parents made sure that each year, during the holiday season, the family was together, and we had fun! During the Christmas season, we participated in various activities. Most of my siblings played musical instruments, and we were in the school band. It was always a Christmas concert, and I remember how excited I was to see my mom in the audience cheering us on. We had activities at church too, speeches, pageants, wrapping gifts, and making Christmas baskets for everyone. We'd decorate our artificial Christmas tree (I absolutely loved doing this and would be so excited).

My parents bought us toys, and we drove around for hours looking at the holiday lights. During the Thanksgiving season, I would help my mom in the kitchen, cooking the special meal of our favorite foods, all the while watching the Thanksgiving parade on the TV. Afterward, the family would gather around the table, give thanks, and enjoy the specialty meal with all the fixings. What was most important was we were building lasting memories and family bonds. Now in a blended family, this can be tricky and challenging because it's not like the nuclear family. For one, the children are not just with their family of origin, but the families are being combined. Their Christmas or Thanksgiving will be totally different. They will have questions about what the holiday will look like, be like, or who they will even be with. Will it be the same?

Will I enjoy it? The stepparents may feel unappreciated in spite of everything they do, and the bio parents may feel like they're stuck in the middle. So I just want to give you some tips to help you navigate through the holiday season with your blended family. The first thing is to prepare for this season. Don't think that this holiday season will be the same as the last holiday season. Remember, in a blended family, everything is fluid, which means that things are constantly changing.

What worked last year may not work this year. Plans may have to change. Secondly, go ahead and do what I just did at the beginning of this segment. Think about your childhood. What did you enjoy about it? What are some things that you want to repeat with your child(ren)?

What are some things that you don't want to repeat? Think about how the season was for you and remember that you want your child(ren) to enjoy it just as much as you did or as much as you wanted to. What I'm saying is, "remember your childhood." Next, the stress of the holidays can cause major conflict with the ex-partner. Whether it's they don't want to share the kids, they don't want to change their schedule, they don't want to follow the parental agreement, they are jealous of you and your partner, they are in competition with you, and whatever the reason, just know it can disrupt the holiday. You know your ex-partner better than anyone. You know what causes them to get upset. So if you think something may cause an argument, choose your battles wisely.

You can control yourself, but you can't control what your ex thinks or feels. So don't get upset if they don't do what you think should be done or say things the way you think they should be said; you cannot control them. Ask yourself during this season, "Do I want to make it enjoyable for my child(ren)? If so, how can I do it? "How can I be flexible?" and "What are some things that I can do to make it better for them?" But in spite of everything that you do, the holiday schedules just may not work and may not be able to be altered. Now is a time for you to be creative and make new memories and new traditions.

In my blended family, this was a lesson we learned. Many times, it was just too much of a challenge to consistently get my bonus kids on the holidays; their mom wanted the kids to be with her. Even if that time fell on my husband's scheduled time, it still posed a challenge. We had to be creative, so the new tradition we created was we spent the holiday eve or two days before the holiday together. That worked out perfectly. As a matter of fact, we still do that tradition today.

My kids are all grown up, and some of them have families of their own. It works out because now they don't feel the pressures of splitting their holidays with us and other family members' homes. I want to encourage you to think about the holiday season and how it affects your kids. Is it the best or one with stress? Maya Angelo summed it up very nicely. She said people might not remember what you said. People may not remember what you did, but people will always remember how you made them feel. How do you want your child(ren) to feel during the holidays?

# REFLECTION QUESTIONS

*Be completely humble and gentle; be patient, bearing
one another in love. Make every effort to keep unity
of the Spirit through the bond of peace.*
—Ephesians 4:2–3

What unique challenges does your blended family experience during the holiday season? How have you addressed it? Has it been successful?

_____

_____

_____

_____

_____

_____

_____

_____

_____

_____

Is the current way you handle the holidays creating wonderful memories for your child(ren)? What makes you think this?

_____

_____

_____

_____

_____

_____

_____

_____

_____

_____

Are there new experiences and traditions you can start in your blended family?

_____

_____

_____

_____

_____

_____

_____

_____

_____

_____

How will this improve the holiday season for your family?

_____

_____

_____

_____

_____

_____

_____

_____

_____

_____

# CHAPTER 13

## How Do I Refocus

"My partner's parents treat my kids differently than their other bio grandkids, they're evil, mean, and just hateful people! And I don't want to be around them!" I can't tell you how many times I've heard this statement, seen it written, or even experienced it myself. I don't have to address if it's right or wrong because, obviously, we know that all children should be treated fairly in a family. But I want to look at what could be going on in those situations. Now I know some individuals will stop reading or start protesting, "I don't care what's going on because they are just kids, and they don't deserve to be treated that way!" You're absolutely 100 percent right on both points.

But I always say before you jump to a conclusion, you have to know the back story. Meaning, how did we get here? Sometimes when you understand "the why," it changes the perspective of how you're looking at it. Let's look at your response. The reason you are so passionate about how you feel is that they are your child(ren). You are like a "mama or papa bear" wanting to protect your children from all and any hurt. It's not that you are a mean and hateful person, but when it comes to your child(ren), you will take a stand and handle whatever comes with it. The very first thing I want to say is the way you feel is absolutely correct, Miss Mama Bear or Mister Papa Bear. You are protecting your child, and just like a mama bear and papa bear with their little cub, anybody that comes toward them to harm will attack. Likewise, whoever comes for your child, you are going to jump into protective mode. You don't want them to feel neglected or unwanted. It's absolutely *okay* for you to feel that way. So own your feelings. Many times that gets missed in the conversation, and you may feel others don't understand why you are angry. Your first instinct is to protect your child, so understand and own that because that is why you feel like that.

Now a couple of these points I am going to reference might be a little difficult to process, but just hear me out. You have just gotten into this relationship with your partner and been in it for maybe three months (I know of couples in their relationship for a shorter period of time, three weeks or even a month), and you have moved in together, and "you see yourself as a family" and want everyone else to see you as "family." Well, your partner's family knows him and may feel they have a habit of getting in and out of relationships. It's a pattern, so they may want to sit back and wait to see if this is going to be more permanent.

You just got into the relationship and may not understand your partner has a habit of being in different relationships, and by the time the family really gets to know that person, they've moved on to someone else. Your partner's family may be cautious about who they call family. So take a step back and look at this situation. Another point to consider is you may be rushing things. By that, I mean it takes time for relationships to form, and you want them to develop quicker (I can relate to this because I felt like this many times). But in the blended family, it will take time for you to bond with your stepkids, and it takes time for the grandparents to bond too. They have been with their bio grandchildren for years.

When they knew that their loved one was expecting, they started visualizing the type of grandparent they wanted to be, and the acceptance and bonding process started then. While the baby was developing in the womb, they started visualizing how their relationship with their grandchild would be. Then when the baby was born, it became real, and they felt the joy and excitement of being a grandparent. Now the child is five or six years old, and they had all those years of bonding with them. Now you are here with your kids expecting the bond to happen quickly. Some people's personalities are warm and inviting, and they make you feel comfortable when you are around them. They do that with everyone. You think their inviting personality shows they love your kids right away. But when you realize they don't, you get angry. I put this in here because I've had clients say, "They liked my kids at first, and then things changed." Don't get a pleasant personality confused with loving someone. It takes time for the bond to happen. Also, some people still hold strongly to the belief that couples should be married before accepting them as family.

While you may not subscribe to this belief, your partner's family may. You have a right to your belief, and they do too. Even though they may feel like that now, over time, things may change. So try not to take it personally. Lastly, they may be grieving the last relationship. They may have had a bond with the last person and really liked them. They invested time in building up the relationship and had expectations for the future, and now it is over. So they are grieving it. They may even be upset at how it ended, and it is not even about you. You just happen to be in their line of fire. So again, this is about looking at the situation and giving it time and realizing things are not going to just jump right into place. These are just a few reasons why there may be challenges with your partner's family.

Now, if you have been in the relationship for over five years, and they still haven't accepted your children, something else might be going on. But in the early years, these may be the extenuating circumstances. When you're confronting the situation, please don't make threats like "If you don't like me or accept my kids, you can't come to my house, or I'm not going to let any of the kids go to your house." The best way to address this for your partner or your spouse is to get on the same page.

Remember, they are your partner's parents, so they may not automatically see things the way you see them. Don't be upset and get angry if they don't see your viewpoint right away. Remember, the goal is to be on the same page and not for them to be as angry as you are about it. They may agree that this is something that needs to be addressed, so once you get them on the same page, then the issue can be addressed.

Now you may not be able to approach them because you have built up so many emotions and might not be in the best place to be kind with your words. So let your partner address it. After all, it's their parents, and they know them much better than you. You don't want to say or do things that will make it worse. Be mindful that the situation may change, or it may not change; be ready for that. The only thing that you can do is make sure that in your home, you are treating all the kids fairly. There are some things that you can control and some things that you cannot control, and that's just one aspect of a blended family that you have to be prepared for.

# REFLECTION QUESTIONS

*If it is possible, as far as it depends on you, live at peace with everyone.*
—Romans 12:18

Do you feel that your partner's family demonstrates a difference with the children? If so, how has this affected you, your child(ren), and the relationship?

_____

_____

_____

_____

_____

_____

_____

_____

_____

_____

Has your partner addressed the concerns with their family? If so, what was the response? If not, why not?

_____

_____

_____

_____

_____

_____

_____

_____

_____

_____

What things can you do to create a supportive and inclusive environment for all the children in your home?

_____
_____
_____
_____
_____
_____
_____
_____
_____
_____
_____

How will this help improve your blended family relationship?

_____
_____
_____
_____
_____
_____
_____
_____
_____
_____

# ABOUT THE AUTHOR

Lois Goudeau is a Christian, a special education teacher, a licensed clinical professional counselor, and a transformation coach. She has been in a blended family for twenty-seven years and has worked with hundreds of clients in various blended family situations. Utilizing her personal and life experiences along with clinical skills, she has created a coaching program called Mosaic Transformation Academy. In her coaching program, she helps stepparents have open and effective communication without feeling like an outsider, a third wheel, resentful, or isolated in their blended family relationship.

Her passion to help stepparents can be seen weekly on her YouTube channel "Ask Lois the Relatable Therapist."

Lois and her husband, Russell, reside in Illinois. They have a blended family of five children, one son-in-law, and six grandchildren.

Contact information: askcoachlois@gmail.com
MTA Coaching: https://workshop-signup-7435.ck.page/dce8d5a261
YouTube Channel (Ask Lois The Relatable Therapist): https://www.
youtube.com/@askloistherelatabletherapist

Thanks for reading my book; I hope you found it useful as it helps you on your unique journey to blending your family! If you did, please leave a review on the site where you purchased the book. Thank you so much!